this journal
BELONGS TO

A TRIBUTE TO A TRAILBLAZER

Born on October 20, 1964, in Oakland, California, Kamala Harris was elected the first woman, first African American, and first Asian American to serve as Vice President of the United States of America. Never one to back down from a fight, Harris has dedicated her life to fighting for truth, equality, and justice. After studying political science and economics and graduating from Howard University, Harris went on to earn a law degree from Hastings College. Harris then began a legal career in the Alameda County District Attorney's office, earning a reputation for toughness as she prosecuted cases of gang violence, drug trafficking, and sexual abuse. Harris rose through the ranks and in 2010, was elected attorney general of California, becoming the first woman and the first African American to hold the position. Widely considered a rising star within the Democratic party, Harris was recruited to run for the U.S. Senate election in California. Among her many successes, Harris defended California's landmark climate change law, protected the Affordable Care Act, helped win marriage equality for all Californians, and addressed increases to minimum wage. She easily won the Senate election in 2016. When Joe Biden chose her as his running mate in the 2020 presidential race, Harris became the fourth woman to appear on a major political party's presidential ticket and the first to win, having risen higher in United States leadership than any woman before her.

Known for her fierce leadership and unwavering determination over the course of her groundbreaking career, Harris has shattered countless glass ceilings for women and people of color everywhere. This journal is dedicated to Kamala Harris, the extraordinary women like her, and "every little girl watching."

"ANYONE WHO CLAIMS TO BE A LEADER MUST SPEAK LIKE A LEADER. THAT MEANS SPEAKING WITH INTEGRITY AND TRUTH."

—KAMALA HARRIS

"I'M SPEAKING."

—KAMALA HARRIS

"WHILE I MAY BE THE
FIRST WOMAN
IN THIS OFFICE,
I WILL NOT BE THE LAST
BECAUSE EVERY LITTLE GIRL
WATCHING TONIGHT SEES
THAT THIS IS A COUNTRY
OF POSSIBILITIES."

—KAMALA HARRIS

"HERE'S THE TRUTH PEOPLE
NEED TO UNDERSTAND: TO
TACKLE THE CHALLENGES OF
THE TWENTY-FIRST CENTURY,
WE MUST **EMPOWER** WOMEN
AND FAMILIES. IF WE DO NOT
LIFT UP WOMEN AND FAMILIES,
EVERYONE WILL FALL SHORT."

—KAMALA HARRIS

"OUR UNITY IS
OUR **STRENGTH**, AND OUR
DIVERSITY IS OUR **POWER**.
WE REJECT THE
MYTH OF 'US' VS.
'THEM.' WE ARE
IN THIS **TOGETHER**."

—KAMALA HARRIS

"THERE **WILL** BE A RESISTANCE TO YOUR **AMBITION**, THERE **WILL** BE PEOPLE WHO SAY TO YOU, 'YOU ARE OUT OF YOUR LANE.' THEY ARE BURDENED BY ONLY HAVING THE CAPACITY TO SEE WHAT HAS ALWAYS BEEN INSTEAD OF **WHAT CAN BE.** BUT DON'T LET THAT BURDEN **YOU.**"

—KAMALA HARRIS

"WHAT I WANT YOUNG
WOMEN AND GIRLS TO KNOW
IS: YOU ARE **POWERFUL**
AND YOUR VOICE MATTERS."

—KAMALA HARRIS

"NEVER ASK ANYONE'S
PERMISSION TO LEAD.
JUST LEAD."

—KAMALA HARRIS

"THE AMERICAN DREAM BELONGS TO ALL OF US."

—KAMALA HARRIS

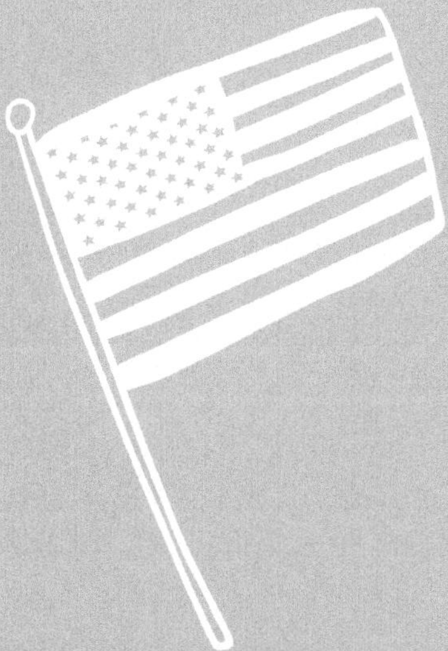

"A **PATRIOT** IS NOT SOMEONE WHO CONDONES THE CONDUCT OF OUR COUNTRY, WHATEVER IT DOES; IT IS SOMEONE WHO **FIGHTS** EVERY DAY FOR THE IDEALS OF THE COUNTRY, **WHATEVER IT TAKES.**"

—KAMALA HARRIS

"YOU HAVE TO SEE
AND SMELL AND FEEL
THE CIRCUMSTANCES
OF PEOPLE TO REALLY
UNDERSTAND THEM."

—KAMALA HARRIS

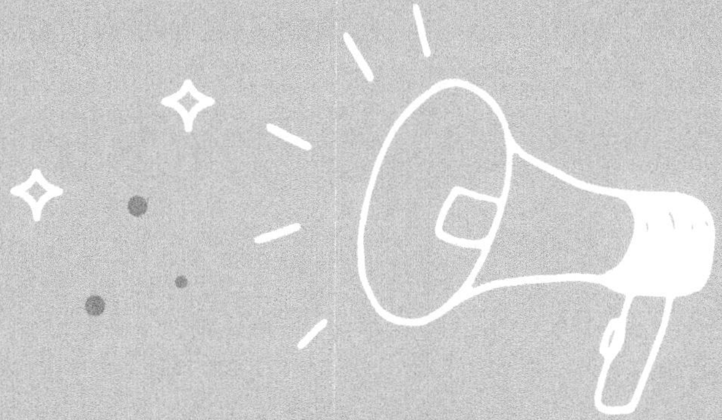

"NO LONGER CAN SOME
WAIT ON THE SIDELINES,
HOPING FOR
INCREMENTAL CHANGE.
IN TIMES LIKE THIS,
SILENCE IS COMPLICITY."

—KAMALA HARRIS

"I AM WHO I AM."

—KAMALA HARRIS

"THERE IS NO VACCINE
FOR RACISM. WE'VE
GOTTA **DO THE WORK**.
FOR GEORGE FLOYD. FOR
BREONNA TAYLOR. FOR THE
LIVES OF TOO MANY OTHERS
TO NAME. FOR OUR CHILDREN.
FOR **ALL OF US**."

—KAMALA HARRIS

This publication is designed to provide accurate and authoritative information in regard to
the subject matter covered. It is sold with the understanding that the publisher is not engaged
in rendering legal, accounting, or other professional service. If legal advice or other expert
assistance is required, the services of a competent professional person should be sought.
—From a Declaration of Principles Jointly Adopted by a Committee of the American Bar
Association and a Committee of Publishers and Associations

Published by Sourcebooks
P.O. Box 4410, Naperville, Illinois 60567-4410
(630) 961-3900
sourcebooks.com

Printed and bound in the United States of America.
POD

Made in the USA
Monee, IL
23 January 2021

56802327R00066